THE TRAINSPOTTER'S LOG BOOK

By Dan Oldfield

First Printed 2018
Printed ISBN 978-1-9160097-0-7

PINBROOK
PUBLISHING

THE TRAINSPOTTER'S LOG BOOK

Introduction

Train spotting is regarded as a hobby and mainly involves the collection in sightings of trains. Many enthusiasts will keep an eye out for a certain type, category, make or model.

The beginnings of train spotting can be traced back to the dawn of the railways. However, popularity of the hobby took hold in the 1930s. It was the era of fast, streamlined, steam locomotives and when the renowned Mallard took the steam record reaching 126 mph. The locomotives of this period presented an image of luxury and elegance, providing a glamourous way to travel.

The hobby of train spotting firmly established itself in 1942. It was Ian Allen who worked, in the public relations department, for Southern Railway who thought of the idea of creating a booklet providing further information on locomotives, after receiving and answering the many request from rail enthusiast who wanted to know everything there was about the trains.

After his initial idea of collecting data and issuing a publication was rejected by bosses, he decided to take on the task himself. He subsequently went on to release his first booklet "ABC of Southern Locomotives". This publication proved to be a big success and resulted in the contribution of making trainspotting a very popular hobby.

INSTRUCTIONS

Below is an example on how to fill in the log book.

The location section provides an area where you can record details of the place that you will be monitoring locomotives. Fields include the arrival and end time, the total time spent at the location, the railway line which you will be recording data, name of place and county.

The Rolling Stock section provides an area to log important information related to the locomotive.

DATE ▶ 10th Jan 2019   M (T) W T F S S

LOCATION

Start Time: 3:15 am

End Time: 5:00 pm

Elapsed Time: 1 hr 45 min

Railway Line: Bristol to Exeter Line

Location: Exeter St Davids

County: Devon

ROLLING STOCK

Operator: GWR

Number: 800009

Name: John Charles

Type: DMU

Category: Inter-city

Class: 802

Builder: Hitachi

Year Built: 2018

Carriages: 9

Livery: Dark Green

Operator:

Number:

Name:

Type:

Category:

Class:

Builder:

Year Built:

Carriages:

Livery:

LOCATION

Start Time:

End Time:

Elapsed Time:

Railway Line:

Location:

County:

ROLLING STOCK

Operator:

Number:

Name:

Type:

Category:

Class:

Builder:

Year Built:

Carriages:

Livery:

Operator:

Number:

Name:

Type:

Category:

Class:

Builder:

Year Built:

Carriages:

Livery:

Operator:

Number:

Name:

Type:

Category:

Class:

Builder:

Year Built:

Carriages:

Livery:

Operator: Number:

Name: Type:

Category: Class:

Builder: Year Built:

Carriages: Livery:

Operator: Number:

Name: Type:

Category: Class:

Builder: Year Built:

Carriages: Livery:

Operator: Number:

Name: Type:

Category: Class:

Builder: Year Built:

Carriages: Livery:

Operator: Number:

Name: Type:

Category: Class:

Builder: Year Built:

Carriages: Livery:

Operator: Number:

Name: Type:

Category: Class:

Builder: Year Built:

Carriages: Livery:

Operator: Number:

Name: Type:

Category: Class:

Builder: Year Built:

Carriages: Livery:

Operator: Number:

Name: Type:

Category: Class:

Builder: Year Built:

Carriages: Livery:

Operator: Number:

Name: Type:

Category: Class:

Builder: Year Built:

Carriages: Livery:

NOTES

M T W T F S S

LOCATION

Start Time: End Time:

Elapsed Time: Railway Line:

Location: County:

ROLLING STOCK

Operator: Number:

Name: Type:

Category: Class:

Builder: Year Built:

Carriages: Livery:

Operator: Number:

Name: Type:

Category: Class:

Builder: Year Built:

Carriages: Livery:

Operator: Number:

Name: Type:

Category: Class:

Builder: Year Built:

Carriages: Livery:

Operator: | Number:

Name: | Type:

Category: | Class:

Builder: | Year Built:

Carriages: | Livery:

Operator: | Number:

Name: | Type:

Category: | Class:

Builder: | Year Built:

Carriages: | Livery:

Operator: | Number:

Name: | Type:

Category: | Class:

Builder: | Year Built:

Carriages: | Livery:

Operator: | Number:

Name: | Type:

Category: | Class:

Builder: | Year Built:

Carriages: | Livery:

Operator: Number:

Name: Type:

Category: Class:

Builder: Year Built:

Carriages: Livery:

Operator: Number:

Name: Type:

Category: Class:

Builder: Year Built:

Carriages: Livery:

Operator: Number:

Name: Type:

Category: Class:

Builder: Year Built:

Carriages: Livery:

Operator: Number:

Name: Type:

Category: Class:

Builder: Year Built:

Carriages: Livery:

NOTES

LOCATION

Start Time: End Time:

Elapsed Time: Railway Line:

Location: County:

ROLLING STOCK

Operator: Number:

Name: Type:

Category: Class:

Builder: Year Built:

Carriages: Livery:

Operator: Number:

Name: Type:

Category: Class:

Builder: Year Built:

Carriages: Livery:

Operator: Number:

Name: Type:

Category: Class:

Builder: Year Built:

Carriages: Livery:

Operator: Number:

Name: Type:

Category: Class:

Builder: Year Built:

Carriages: Livery:

Operator: Number:

Name: Type:

Category: Class:

Builder: Year Built:

Carriages: Livery:

Operator: Number:

Name: Type:

Category: Class:

Builder: Year Built:

Carriages: Livery:

Operator: Number:

Name: Type:

Category: Class:

Builder: Year Built:

Carriages: Livery:

Operator: Number:

Name: Type:

Category: Class:

Builder: Year Built:

Carriages: Livery:

Operator: Number:

Name: Type:

Category: Class:

Builder: Year Built:

Carriages: Livery:

Operator: Number:

Name: Type:

Category: Class:

Builder: Year Built:

Carriages: Livery:

Operator: Number:

Name: Type:

Category: Class:

Builder: Year Built:

Carriages: Livery:

NOTES

M   T   W   T   F   S   S

LOCATION

Start Time:

End Time:

Elapsed Time:

Railway Line:

Location:

County:

ROLLING STOCK

Operator:

Number:

Name:

Type:

Category:

Class:

Builder:

Year Built:

Carriages:

Livery:

Operator:

Number:

Name:

Type:

Category:

Class:

Builder:

Year Built:

Carriages:

Livery:

Operator:

Number:

Name:

Type:

Category:

Class:

Builder:

Year Built:

Carriages:

Livery:

Operator: Number:

Name: Type:

Category: Class:

Builder: Year Built:

Carriages: Livery:

Operator: Number:

Name: Type:

Category: Class:

Builder: Year Built:

Carriages: Livery:

Operator: Number:

Name: Type:

Category: Class:

Builder: Year Built:

Carriages: Livery:

Operator: Number:

Name: Type:

Category: Class:

Builder: Year Built:

Carriages: Livery:

Operator: Number:

Name: Type:

Category: Class:

Builder: Year Built:

Carriages: Livery:

Operator: Number:

Name: Type:

Category: Class:

Builder: Year Built:

Carriages: Livery:

Operator: Number:

Name: Type:

Category: Class:

Builder: Year Built:

Carriages: Livery:

Operator: Number:

Name: Type:

Category: Class:

Builder: Year Built:

Carriages: Livery:

NOTES

LOCATION

Start Time: End Time:

Elapsed Time: Railway Line:

Location: County:

ROLLING STOCK

Operator: Number:

Name: Type:

Category: Class:

Builder: Year Built:

Carriages: Livery:

Operator: Number:

Name: Type:

Category: Class:

Builder: Year Built:

Carriages: Livery:

Operator: Number:

Name: Type:

Category: Class:

Builder: Year Built:

Carriages: Livery:

Operator:	Number:
Name:	Type:
Category:	Class:
Builder:	Year Built:
Carriages:	Livery:

Operator:	Number:
Name:	Type:
Category:	Class:
Builder:	Year Built:
Carriages:	Livery:

Operator:	Number:
Name:	Type:
Category:	Class:
Builder:	Year Built:
Carriages:	Livery:

Operator:	Number:
Name:	Type:
Category:	Class:
Builder:	Year Built:
Carriages:	Livery:

Operator: Number:

Name: Type:

Category: Class:

Builder: Year Built:

Carriages: Livery:

Operator: Number:

Name: Type:

Category: Class:

Builder: Year Built:

Carriages: Livery:

Operator: Number:

Name: Type:

Category: Class:

Builder: Year Built:

Carriages: Livery:

Operator: Number:

Name: Type:

Category: Class:

Builder: Year Built:

Carriages: Livery:

NOTES

LOCATION

Start Time: End Time:

Elapsed Time: Railway Line:

Location: County:

ROLLING STOCK

Operator: Number:

Name: Type:

Category: Class:

Builder: Year Built:

Carriages: Livery:

Operator: Number:

Name: Type:

Category: Class:

Builder: Year Built:

Carriages: Livery:

Operator: Number:

Name: Type:

Category: Class:

Builder: Year Built:

Carriages: Livery:

Operator: Number:

Name: Type:

Category: Class:

Builder: Year Built:

Carriages: Livery:

Operator: Number:

Name: Type:

Category: Class:

Builder: Year Built:

Carriages: Livery:

Operator: Number:

Name: Type:

Category: Class:

Builder: Year Built:

Carriages: Livery:

Operator: Number:

Name: Type:

Category: Class:

Builder: Year Built:

Carriages: Livery:

Operator: | Number:

Name: | Type:

Category: | Class:

Builder: | Year Built:

Carriages: | Livery:

Operator: | Number:

Name: | Type:

Category: | Class:

Builder: | Year Built:

Carriages: | Livery:

Operator: | Number:

Name: | Type:

Category: | Class:

Builder: | Year Built:

Carriages: | Livery:

Operator: | Number:

Name: | Type:

Category: | Class:

Builder: | Year Built:

Carriages: | Livery:

NOTES

M T W T F S S

LOCATION

Start Time:

End Time:

Elapsed Time:

Railway Line:

Location:

County:

ROLLING STOCK

Operator:

Number:

Name:

Type:

Category:

Class:

Builder:

Year Built:

Carriages:

Livery:

Operator:

Number:

Name:

Type:

Category:

Class:

Builder:

Year Built:

Carriages:

Livery:

Operator:

Number:

Name:

Type:

Category:

Class:

Builder:

Year Built:

Carriages:

Livery:

Operator: | Number:

Name: | Type:

Category: | Class:

Builder: | Year Built:

Carriages: | Livery:

Operator: | Number:

Name: | Type:

Category: | Class:

Builder: | Year Built:

Carriages: | Livery:

Operator: | Number:

Name: | Type:

Category: | Class:

Builder: | Year Built:

Carriages: | Livery:

Operator: | Number:

Name: | Type:

Category: | Class:

Builder: | Year Built:

Carriages: | Livery:

Operator: Number:

Name: Type:

Category: Class:

Builder: Year Built:

Carriages: Livery:

Operator: Number:

Name: Type:

Category: Class:

Builder: Year Built:

Carriages: Livery:

Operator: Number:

Name: Type:

Category: Class:

Builder: Year Built:

Carriages: Livery:

Operator: Number:

Name: Type:

Category: Class:

Builder: Year Built:

Carriages: Livery:

NOTES

DATE

LOCATION

Start Time:

End Time:

Elapsed Time:

Railway Line:

Location:

County:

ROLLING STOCK

Operator:

Number:

Name:

Type:

Category:

Class:

Builder:

Year Built:

Carriages:

Livery:

Operator:

Number:

Name:

Type:

Category:

Class:

Builder:

Year Built:

Carriages:

Livery:

Operator:

Number:

Name:

Type:

Category:

Class:

Builder:

Year Built:

Carriages:

Livery:

Operator: | Number:

Name: | Type:

Category: | Class:

Builder: | Year Built:

Carriages: | Livery:

Operator: | Number:

Name: | Type:

Category: | Class:

Builder: | Year Built:

Carriages: | Livery:

Operator: | Number:

Name: | Type:

Category: | Class:

Builder: | Year Built:

Carriages: | Livery:

Operator: | Number:

Name: | Type:

Category: | Class:

Builder: | Year Built:

Carriages: | Livery:

Operator: Number:

Name: Type:

Category: Class:

Builder: Year Built:

Carriages: Livery:

Operator: Number:

Name: Type:

Category: Class:

Builder: Year Built:

Carriages: Livery:

Operator: Number:

Name: Type:

Category: Class:

Builder: Year Built:

Carriages: Livery:

Operator: Number:

Name: Type:

Category: Class:

Builder: Year Built:

Carriages: Livery:

NOTES

LOCATION

Start Time:

End Time:

Elapsed Time:

Railway Line:

Location:

County:

ROLLING STOCK

Operator:

Number:

Name:

Type:

Category:

Class:

Builder:

Year Built:

Carriages:

Livery:

Operator:

Number:

Name:

Type:

Category:

Class:

Builder:

Year Built:

Carriages:

Livery:

Operator:

Number:

Name:

Type:

Category:

Class:

Builder:

Year Built:

Carriages:

Livery:

Operator: Number:

Name: Type:

Category: Class:

Builder: Year Built:

Carriages: Livery:

Operator: Number:

Name: Type:

Category: Class:

Builder: Year Built:

Carriages: Livery:

Operator: Number:

Name: Type:

Category: Class:

Builder: Year Built:

Carriages: Livery:

Operator: Number:

Name: Type:

Category: Class:

Builder: Year Built:

Carriages: Livery:

CONT.

Operator: Number:

Name: Type:

Category: Class:

Builder: Year Built:

Carriages: Livery:

Operator: Number:

Name: Type:

Category: Class:

Builder: Year Built:

Carriages: Livery:

Operator: Number:

Name: Type:

Category: Class:

Builder: Year Built:

Carriages: Livery:

Operator: Number:

Name: Type:

Category: Class:

Builder: Year Built:

Carriages: Livery:

NOTES

LOCATION

Start Time: End Time:

Elapsed Time: Railway Line:

Location: County:

ROLLING STOCK

Operator: Number:

Name: Type:

Category: Class:

Builder: Year Built:

Carriages: Livery:

Operator: Number:

Name: Type:

Category: Class:

Builder: Year Built:

Carriages: Livery:

Operator: Number:

Name: Type:

Category: Class:

Builder: Year Built:

Carriages: Livery:

Operator: Number:

Name: Type:

Category: Class:

Builder: Year Built:

Carriages: Livery:

Operator: Number:

Name: Type:

Category: Class:

Builder: Year Built:

Carriages: Livery:

Operator: Number:

Name: Type:

Category: Class:

Builder: Year Built:

Carriages: Livery:

Operator: Number:

Name: Type:

Category: Class:

Builder: Year Built:

Carriages: Livery:

Operator: Number:

Name: Type:

Category: Class:

Builder: Year Built:

Carriages: Livery:

Operator: Number:

Name: Type:

Category: Class:

Builder: Year Built:

Carriages: Livery:

Operator: Number:

Name: Type:

Category: Class:

Builder: Year Built:

Carriages: Livery:

Operator: Number:

Name: Type:

Category: Class:

Builder: Year Built:

Carriages: Livery:

NOTES

LOCATION

Start Time: End Time:

Elapsed Time: Railway Line:

Location: County:

ROLLING STOCK

Operator: Number:

Name: Type:

Category: Class:

Builder: Year Built:

Carriages: Livery:

Operator: Number:

Name: Type:

Category: Class:

Builder: Year Built:

Carriages: Livery:

Operator: Number:

Name: Type:

Category: Class:

Builder: Year Built:

Carriages: Livery:

Operator: Number:

Name: Type:

Category: Class:

Builder: Year Built:

Carriages: Livery:

Operator: Number:

Name: Type:

Category: Class:

Builder: Year Built:

Carriages: Livery:

Operator: Number:

Name: Type:

Category: Class:

Builder: Year Built:

Carriages: Livery:

Operator: Number:

Name: Type:

Category: Class:

Builder: Year Built:

Carriages: Livery:

Operator: | Number:

Name: | Type:

Category: | Class:

Builder: | Year Built:

Carriages: | Livery:

Operator: | Number:

Name: | Type:

Category: | Class:

Builder: | Year Built:

Carriages: | Livery:

Operator: | Number:

Name: | Type:

Category: | Class:

Builder: | Year Built:

Carriages: | Livery:

Operator: | Number:

Name: | Type:

Category: | Class:

Builder: | Year Built:

Carriages: | Livery:

NOTES

M T W T F S S

LOCATION

Start Time: End Time:

Elapsed Time: Railway Line:

Location: County:

ROLLING STOCK

Operator: Number:

Name: Type:

Category: Class:

Builder: Year Built:

Carriages: Livery:

Operator: Number:

Name: Type:

Category: Class:

Builder: Year Built:

Carriages: Livery:

Operator: Number:

Name: Type:

Category: Class:

Builder: Year Built:

Carriages: Livery:

Operator: Number:

Name: Type:

Category: Class:

Builder: Year Built:

Carriages: Livery:

Operator: Number:

Name: Type:

Category: Class:

Builder: Year Built:

Carriages: Livery:

Operator: Number:

Name: Type:

Category: Class:

Builder: Year Built:

Carriages: Livery:

Operator: Number:

Name: Type:

Category: Class:

Builder: Year Built:

Carriages: Livery:

Operator: Number:

Name: Type:

Category: Class:

Builder: Year Built:

Carriages: Livery:

Operator: Number:

Name: Type:

Category: Class:

Builder: Year Built:

Carriages: Livery:

Operator: Number:

Name: Type:

Category: Class:

Builder: Year Built:

Carriages: Livery:

Operator: Number:

Name: Type:

Category: Class:

Builder: Year Built:

Carriages: Livery:

NOTES

LOCATION

Start Time: End Time:

Elapsed Time: Railway Line:

Location: County:

ROLLING STOCK

Operator: Number:

Name: Type:

Category: Class:

Builder: Year Built:

Carriages: Livery:

Operator: Number:

Name: Type:

Category: Class:

Builder: Year Built:

Carriages: Livery:

Operator: Number:

Name: Type:

Category: Class:

Builder: Year Built:

Carriages: Livery:

Operator: Number:

Name: Type:

Category: Class:

Builder: Year Built:

Carriages: Livery:

Operator: Number:

Name: Type:

Category: Class:

Builder: Year Built:

Carriages: Livery:

Operator: Number:

Name: Type:

Category: Class:

Builder: Year Built:

Carriages: Livery:

Operator: Number:

Name: Type:

Category: Class:

Builder: Year Built:

Carriages: Livery:

Operator: Number:

Name: Type:

Category: Class:

Builder: Year Built:

Carriages: Livery:

Operator: Number:

Name: Type:

Category: Class:

Builder: Year Built:

Carriages: Livery:

Operator: Number:

Name: Type:

Category: Class:

Builder: Year Built:

Carriages: Livery:

Operator: Number:

Name: Type:

Category: Class:

Builder: Year Built:

Carriages: Livery:

NOTES

LOCATION

Start Time:

End Time:

Elapsed Time:

Railway Line:

Location:

County:

ROLLING STOCK

Operator:

Number:

Name:

Type:

Category:

Class:

Builder:

Year Built:

Carriages:

Livery:

Operator:

Number:

Name:

Type:

Category:

Class:

Builder:

Year Built:

Carriages:

Livery:

Operator:

Number:

Name:

Type:

Category:

Class:

Builder:

Year Built:

Carriages:

Livery:

Operator: Number:

Name: Type:

Category: Class:

Builder: Year Built:

Carriages: Livery:

Operator: Number:

Name: Type:

Category: Class:

Builder: Year Built:

Carriages: Livery:

Operator: Number:

Name: Type:

Category: Class:

Builder: Year Built:

Carriages: Livery:

Operator: Number:

Name: Type:

Category: Class:

Builder: Year Built:

Carriages: Livery:

Operator: Number:

Name: Type:

Category: Class:

Builder: Year Built:

Carriages: Livery:

Operator: Number:

Name: Type:

Category: Class:

Builder: Year Built:

Carriages: Livery:

Operator: Number:

Name: Type:

Category: Class:

Builder: Year Built:

Carriages: Livery:

Operator: Number:

Name: Type:

Category: Class:

Builder: Year Built:

Carriages: Livery:

NOTES

M T W T F S S

LOCATION

Start Time: End Time:

Elapsed Time: Railway Line:

Location: County:

ROLLING STOCK

Operator: Number:

Name: Type:

Category: Class:

Builder: Year Built:

Carriages: Livery:

Operator: Number:

Name: Type:

Category: Class:

Builder: Year Built:

Carriages: Livery:

Operator: Number:

Name: Type:

Category: Class:

Builder: Year Built:

Carriages: Livery:

Operator: Number:

Name: Type:

Category: Class:

Builder: Year Built:

Carriages: Livery:

Operator: Number:

Name: Type:

Category: Class:

Builder: Year Built:

Carriages: Livery:

Operator: Number:

Name: Type:

Category: Class:

Builder: Year Built:

Carriages: Livery:

Operator: Number:

Name: Type:

Category: Class:

Builder: Year Built:

Carriages: Livery:

Operator: Number:

Name: Type:

Category: Class:

Builder: Year Built:

Carriages: Livery:

Operator: Number:

Name: Type:

Category: Class:

Builder: Year Built:

Carriages: Livery:

Operator: Number:

Name: Type:

Category: Class:

Builder: Year Built:

Carriages: Livery:

Operator: Number:

Name: Type:

Category: Class:

Builder: Year Built:

Carriages: Livery:

NOTES

LOCATION

Start Time: End Time:

Elapsed Time: Railway Line:

Location: County:

ROLLING STOCK

Operator: Number:

Name: Type:

Category: Class:

Builder: Year Built:

Carriages: Livery:

Operator: Number:

Name: Type:

Category: Class:

Builder: Year Built:

Carriages: Livery:

Operator: Number:

Name: Type:

Category: Class:

Builder: Year Built:

Carriages: Livery:

Operator: Number:

Name: Type:

Category: Class:

Builder: Year Built:

Carriages: Livery:

Operator: Number:

Name: Type:

Category: Class:

Builder: Year Built:

Carriages: Livery:

Operator: Number:

Name: Type:

Category: Class:

Builder: Year Built:

Carriages: Livery:

Operator: Number:

Name: Type:

Category: Class:

Builder: Year Built:

Carriages: Livery:

Operator: Number:

Name: Type:

Category: Class:

Builder: Year Built:

Carriages: Livery:

Operator: Number:

Name: Type:

Category: Class:

Builder: Year Built:

Carriages: Livery:

Operator: Number:

Name: Type:

Category: Class:

Builder: Year Built:

Carriages: Livery:

Operator: Number:

Name: Type:

Category: Class:

Builder: Year Built:

Carriages: Livery:

NOTES

LOCATION

Start Time: End Time:

Elapsed Time: Railway Line:

Location: County:

ROLLING STOCK

Operator: Number:

Name: Type:

Category: Class:

Builder: Year Built:

Carriages: Livery:

Operator: Number:

Name: Type:

Category: Class:

Builder: Year Built:

Carriages: Livery:

Operator: Number:

Name: Type:

Category: Class:

Builder: Year Built:

Carriages: Livery:

Operator: | Number:

Name: | Type:

Category: | Class:

Builder: | Year Built:

Carriages: | Livery:

Operator: | Number:

Name: | Type:

Category: | Class:

Builder: | Year Built:

Carriages: | Livery:

Operator: | Number:

Name: | Type:

Category: | Class:

Builder: | Year Built:

Carriages: | Livery:

Operator: | Number:

Name: | Type:

Category: | Class:

Builder: | Year Built:

Carriages: | Livery:

Operator: Number:

Name: Type:

Category: Class:

Builder: Year Built:

Carriages: Livery:

Operator: Number:

Name: Type:

Category: Class:

Builder: Year Built:

Carriages: Livery:

Operator: Number:

Name: Type:

Category: Class:

Builder: Year Built:

Carriages: Livery:

Operator: Number:

Name: Type:

Category: Class:

Builder: Year Built:

Carriages: Livery:

NOTES

M T W T F S S

LOCATION

Start Time: End Time:

Elapsed Time: Railway Line:

Location: County:

ROLLING STOCK

Operator: Number:

Name: Type:

Category: Class:

Builder: Year Built:

Carriages: Livery:

Operator: Number:

Name: Type:

Category: Class:

Builder: Year Built:

Carriages: Livery:

Operator: Number:

Name: Type:

Category: Class:

Builder: Year Built:

Carriages: Livery:

Operator: | Number:

Name: | Type:

Category: | Class:

Builder: | Year Built:

Carriages: | Livery:

Operator: | Number:

Name: | Type:

Category: | Class:

Builder: | Year Built:

Carriages: | Livery:

Operator: | Number:

Name: | Type:

Category: | Class:

Builder: | Year Built:

Carriages: | Livery:

Operator: | Number:

Name: | Type:

Category: | Class:

Builder: | Year Built:

Carriages: | Livery:

Operator: Number:

Name: Type:

Category: Class:

Builder: Year Built:

Carriages: Livery:

Operator: Number:

Name: Type:

Category: Class:

Builder: Year Built:

Carriages: Livery:

Operator: Number:

Name: Type:

Category: Class:

Builder: Year Built:

Carriages: Livery:

Operator: Number:

Name: Type:

Category: Class:

Builder: Year Built:

Carriages: Livery:

NOTES

LOCATION

Start Time: End Time:

Elapsed Time: Railway Line:

Location: County:

ROLLING STOCK

Operator: Number:

Name: Type:

Category: Class:

Builder: Year Built:

Carriages: Livery:

Operator: Number:

Name: Type:

Category: Class:

Builder: Year Built:

Carriages: Livery:

Operator: Number:

Name: Type:

Category: Class:

Builder: Year Built:

Carriages: Livery:

Operator: Number:

Name: Type:

Category: Class:

Builder: Year Built:

Carriages: Livery:

Operator: Number:

Name: Type:

Category: Class:

Builder: Year Built:

Carriages: Livery:

Operator: Number:

Name: Type:

Category: Class:

Builder: Year Built:

Carriages: Livery:

Operator: Number:

Name: Type:

Category: Class:

Builder: Year Built:

Carriages: Livery:

Operator: Number:

Name: Type:

Category: Class:

Builder: Year Built:

Carriages: Livery:

Operator: Number:

Name: Type:

Category: Class:

Builder: Year Built:

Carriages: Livery:

Operator: Number:

Name: Type:

Category: Class:

Builder: Year Built:

Carriages: Livery:

Operator: Number:

Name: Type:

Category: Class:

Builder: Year Built:

Carriages: Livery:

NOTES

LOCATION

Start Time:　　　　　　　　　End Time:

Elapsed Time:　　　　　　　　Railway Line:

Location:　　　　　　　　　　County:

ROLLING STOCK

Operator:　　　　　　　　　　Number:

Name:　　　　　　　　　　　　Type:

Category:　　　　　　　　　　Class:

Builder:　　　　　　　　　　Year Built:

Carriages:　　　　　　　　　Livery:

Operator:　　　　　　　　　　Number:

Name:　　　　　　　　　　　　Type:

Category:　　　　　　　　　　Class:

Builder:　　　　　　　　　　Year Built:

Carriages:　　　　　　　　　Livery:

Operator:　　　　　　　　　　Number:

Name:　　　　　　　　　　　　Type:

Category:　　　　　　　　　　Class:

Builder:　　　　　　　　　　Year Built:

Carriages:　　　　　　　　　Livery:

Operator: Number:

Name: Type:

Category: Class:

Builder: Year Built:

Carriages: Livery:

Operator: Number:

Name: Type:

Category: Class:

Builder: Year Built:

Carriages: Livery:

Operator: Number:

Name: Type:

Category: Class:

Builder: Year Built:

Carriages: Livery:

Operator: Number:

Name: Type:

Category: Class:

Builder: Year Built:

Carriages: Livery:

Operator: | Number:

Name: | Type:

Category: | Class:

Builder: | Year Built:

Carriages: | Livery:

Operator: | Number:

Name: | Type:

Category: | Class:

Builder: | Year Built:

Carriages: | Livery:

Operator: | Number:

Name: | Type:

Category: | Class:

Builder: | Year Built:

Carriages: | Livery:

Operator: | Number:

Name: | Type:

Category: | Class:

Builder: | Year Built:

Carriages: | Livery:

NOTES

LOCATION

Start Time: End Time:

Elapsed Time: Railway Line:

Location: County:

ROLLING STOCK

Operator: Number:

Name: Type:

Category: Class:

Builder: Year Built:

Carriages: Livery:

Operator: Number:

Name: Type:

Category: Class:

Builder: Year Built:

Carriages: Livery:

Operator: Number:

Name: Type:

Category: Class:

Builder: Year Built:

Carriages: Livery:

Operator: | Number:

Name: | Type:

Category: | Class:

Builder: | Year Built:

Carriages: | Livery:

Operator: | Number:

Name: | Type:

Category: | Class:

Builder: | Year Built:

Carriages: | Livery:

Operator: | Number:

Name: | Type:

Category: | Class:

Builder: | Year Built:

Carriages: | Livery:

Operator: | Number:

Name: | Type:

Category: | Class:

Builder: | Year Built:

Carriages: | Livery:

Operator: Number:

Name: Type:

Category: Class:

Builder: Year Built:

Carriages: Livery:

Operator: Number:

Name: Type:

Category: Class:

Builder: Year Built:

Carriages: Livery:

Operator: Number:

Name: Type:

Category: Class:

Builder: Year Built:

Carriages: Livery:

Operator: Number:

Name: Type:

Category: Class:

Builder: Year Built:

Carriages: Livery:

NOTES

LOCATION

Start Time: End Time:

Elapsed Time: Railway Line:

Location: County:

ROLLING STOCK

Operator: Number:

Name: Type:

Category: Class:

Builder: Year Built:

Carriages: Livery:

Operator: Number:

Name: Type:

Category: Class:

Builder: Year Built:

Carriages: Livery:

Operator: Number:

Name: Type:

Category: Class:

Builder: Year Built:

Carriages: Livery:

Operator: Number:

Name: Type:

Category: Class:

Builder: Year Built:

Carriages: Livery:

Operator: Number:

Name: Type:

Category: Class:

Builder: Year Built:

Carriages: Livery:

Operator: Number:

Name: Type:

Category: Class:

Builder: Year Built:

Carriages: Livery:

Operator: Number:

Name: Type:

Category: Class:

Builder: Year Built:

Carriages: Livery:

Operator: | Number:

Name: | Type:

Category: | Class:

Builder: | Year Built:

Carriages: | Livery:

Operator: | Number:

Name: | Type:

Category: | Class:

Builder: | Year Built:

Carriages: | Livery:

Operator: | Number:

Name: | Type:

Category: | Class:

Builder: | Year Built:

Carriages: | Livery:

Operator: | Number:

Name: | Type:

Category: | Class:

Builder: | Year Built:

Carriages: | Livery:

NOTES

LOCATION

Start Time:　　　　　　　End Time:

Elapsed Time:　　　　　　Railway Line:

Location:　　　　　　　　County:

ROLLING STOCK

Operator:　　　　　　　　Number:

Name:　　　　　　　　　　Type:

Category:　　　　　　　　Class:

Builder:　　　　　　　　　Year Built:

Carriages:　　　　　　　　Livery:

Operator:　　　　　　　　Number:

Name:　　　　　　　　　　Type:

Category:　　　　　　　　Class:

Builder:　　　　　　　　　Year Built:

Carriages:　　　　　　　　Livery:

Operator:　　　　　　　　Number:

Name:　　　　　　　　　　Type:

Category:　　　　　　　　Class:

Builder:　　　　　　　　　Year Built:

Carriages:　　　　　　　　Livery:

Operator: | Number:

Name: | Type:

Category: | Class:

Builder: | Year Built:

Carriages: | Livery:

Operator: | Number:

Name: | Type:

Category: | Class:

Builder: | Year Built:

Carriages: | Livery:

Operator: | Number:

Name: | Type:

Category: | Class:

Builder: | Year Built:

Carriages: | Livery:

Operator: | Number:

Name: | Type:

Category: | Class:

Builder: | Year Built:

Carriages: | Livery:

CONT.

Operator: **Number:**

Name: **Type:**

Category: **Class:**

Builder: **Year Built:**

Carriages: **Livery:**

Operator: **Number:**

Name: **Type:**

Category: **Class:**

Builder: **Year Built:**

Carriages: **Livery:**

Operator: **Number:**

Name: **Type:**

Category: **Class:**

Builder: **Year Built:**

Carriages: **Livery:**

Operator: **Number:**

Name: **Type:**

Category: **Class:**

Builder: **Year Built:**

Carriages: **Livery:**

NOTES

LOCATION

Start Time: End Time:

Elapsed Time: Railway Line:

Location: County:

ROLLING STOCK

Operator: Number:

Name: Type:

Category: Class:

Builder: Year Built:

Carriages: Livery:

Operator: Number:

Name: Type:

Category: Class:

Builder: Year Built:

Carriages: Livery:

Operator: Number:

Name: Type:

Category: Class:

Builder: Year Built:

Carriages: Livery:

Operator: | Number:

Name: | Type:

Category: | Class:

Builder: | Year Built:

Carriages: | Livery:

Operator: | Number:

Name: | Type:

Category: | Class:

Builder: | Year Built:

Carriages: | Livery:

Operator: | Number:

Name: | Type:

Category: | Class:

Builder: | Year Built:

Carriages: | Livery:

Operator: | Number:

Name: | Type:

Category: | Class:

Builder: | Year Built:

Carriages: | Livery:

Operator: Number:

Name: Type:

Category: Class:

Builder: Year Built:

Carriages: Livery:

Operator: Number:

Name: Type:

Category: Class:

Builder: Year Built:

Carriages: Livery:

Operator: Number:

Name: Type:

Category: Class:

Builder: Year Built:

Carriages: Livery:

Operator: Number:

Name: Type:

Category: Class:

Builder: Year Built:

Carriages: Livery:

NOTES

LOCATION

Start Time: End Time:

Elapsed Time: Railway Line:

Location: County:

ROLLING STOCK

Operator: Number:

Name: Type:

Category: Class:

Builder: Year Built:

Carriages: Livery:

Operator: Number:

Name: Type:

Category: Class:

Builder: Year Built:

Carriages: Livery:

Operator: Number:

Name: Type:

Category: Class:

Builder: Year Built:

Carriages: Livery:

Operator: Number:

Name: Type:

Category: Class:

Builder: Year Built:

Carriages: Livery:

Operator: Number:

Name: Type:

Category: Class:

Builder: Year Built:

Carriages: Livery:

Operator: Number:

Name: Type:

Category: Class:

Builder: Year Built:

Carriages: Livery:

Operator: Number:

Name: Type:

Category: Class:

Builder: Year Built:

Carriages: Livery:

Operator: Number:

Name: Type:

Category: Class:

Builder: Year Built:

Carriages: Livery:

Operator: Number:

Name: Type:

Category: Class:

Builder: Year Built:

Carriages: Livery:

Operator: Number:

Name: Type:

Category: Class:

Builder: Year Built:

Carriages: Livery:

Operator: Number:

Name: Type:

Category: Class:

Builder: Year Built:

Carriages: Livery:

NOTES

LOCATION

Start Time:　　　　　　　End Time:

Elapsed Time:　　　　　　Railway Line:

Location:　　　　　　　　County:

ROLLING STOCK

Operator:　　　　　　　　Number:

Name:　　　　　　　　　　Type:

Category:　　　　　　　　Class:

Builder:　　　　　　　　　Year Built:

Carriages:　　　　　　　　Livery:

Operator:　　　　　　　　Number:

Name:　　　　　　　　　　Type:

Category:　　　　　　　　Class:

Builder:　　　　　　　　　Year Built:

Carriages:　　　　　　　　Livery:

Operator:　　　　　　　　Number:

Name:　　　　　　　　　　Type:

Category:　　　　　　　　Class:

Builder:　　　　　　　　　Year Built:

Carriages:　　　　　　　　Livery:

Operator: | Number:

Name: | Type:

Category: | Class:

Builder: | Year Built:

Carriages: | Livery:

Operator: | Number:

Name: | Type:

Category: | Class:

Builder: | Year Built:

Carriages: | Livery:

Operator: | Number:

Name: | Type:

Category: | Class:

Builder: | Year Built:

Carriages: | Livery:

Operator: | Number:

Name: | Type:

Category: | Class:

Builder: | Year Built:

Carriages: | Livery:

Operator: Number:

Name: Type:

Category: Class:

Builder: Year Built:

Carriages: Livery:

Operator: Number:

Name: Type:

Category: Class:

Builder: Year Built:

Carriages: Livery:

Operator: Number:

Name: Type:

Category: Class:

Builder: Year Built:

Carriages: Livery:

Operator: Number:

Name: Type:

Category: Class:

Builder: Year Built:

Carriages: Livery:

NOTES

LOCATION

Start Time: End Time:

Elapsed Time: Railway Line:

Location: County:

ROLLING STOCK

Operator: Number:

Name: Type:

Category: Class:

Builder: Year Built:

Carriages: Livery:

Operator: Number:

Name: Type:

Category: Class:

Builder: Year Built:

Carriages: Livery:

Operator: Number:

Name: Type:

Category: Class:

Builder: Year Built:

Carriages: Livery:

Operator: Number:

Name: Type:

Category: Class:

Builder: Year Built:

Carriages: Livery:

Operator: Number:

Name: Type:

Category: Class:

Builder: Year Built:

Carriages: Livery:

Operator: Number:

Name: Type:

Category: Class:

Builder: Year Built:

Carriages: Livery:

Operator: Number:

Name: Type:

Category: Class:

Builder: Year Built:

Carriages: Livery:

Operator: Number:

Name: Type:

Category: Class:

Builder: Year Built:

Carriages: Livery:

Operator: Number:

Name: Type:

Category: Class:

Builder: Year Built:

Carriages: Livery:

Operator: Number:

Name: Type:

Category: Class:

Builder: Year Built:

Carriages: Livery:

Operator: Number:

Name: Type:

Category: Class:

Builder: Year Built:

Carriages: Livery:

NOTES

LOCATION

Start Time: End Time:

Elapsed Time: Railway Line:

Location: County:

ROLLING STOCK

Operator: Number:

Name: Type:

Category: Class:

Builder: Year Built:

Carriages: Livery:

Operator: Number:

Name: Type:

Category: Class:

Builder: Year Built:

Carriages: Livery:

Operator: Number:

Name: Type:

Category: Class:

Builder: Year Built:

Carriages: Livery:

Operator: | Number:

Name: | Type:

Category: | Class:

Builder: | Year Built:

Carriages: | Livery:

Operator: | Number:

Name: | Type:

Category: | Class:

Builder: | Year Built:

Carriages: | Livery:

Operator: | Number:

Name: | Type:

Category: | Class:

Builder: | Year Built:

Carriages: | Livery:

Operator: | Number:

Name: | Type:

Category: | Class:

Builder: | Year Built:

Carriages: | Livery:

Operator: Number:

Name: Type:

Category: Class:

Builder: Year Built:

Carriages: Livery:

Operator: Number:

Name: Type:

Category: Class:

Builder: Year Built:

Carriages: Livery:

Operator: Number:

Name: Type:

Category: Class:

Builder: Year Built:

Carriages: Livery:

Operator: Number:

Name: Type:

Category: Class:

Builder: Year Built:

Carriages: Livery:

NOTES

LOCATION

Start Time: End Time:

Elapsed Time: Railway Line:

Location: County:

ROLLING STOCK

Operator: Number:

Name: Type:

Category: Class:

Builder: Year Built:

Carriages: Livery:

Operator: Number:

Name: Type:

Category: Class:

Builder: Year Built:

Carriages: Livery:

Operator: Number:

Name: Type:

Category: Class:

Builder: Year Built:

Carriages: Livery:

Operator: Number:

Name: Type:

Category: Class:

Builder: Year Built:

Carriages: Livery:

Operator: Number:

Name: Type:

Category: Class:

Builder: Year Built:

Carriages: Livery:

Operator: Number:

Name: Type:

Category: Class:

Builder: Year Built:

Carriages: Livery:

Operator: Number:

Name: Type:

Category: Class:

Builder: Year Built:

Carriages: Livery:

Operator: Number:

Name: Type:

Category: Class:

Builder: Year Built:

Carriages: Livery:

Operator: Number:

Name: Type:

Category: Class:

Builder: Year Built:

Carriages: Livery:

Operator: Number:

Name: Type:

Category: Class:

Builder: Year Built:

Carriages: Livery:

Operator: Number:

Name: Type:

Category: Class:

Builder: Year Built:

Carriages: Livery:

NOTES

DATE

LOCATION

Start Time:

End Time:

Elapsed Time:

Railway Line:

Location:

County:

ROLLING STOCK

Operator:

Number:

Name:

Type:

Category:

Class:

Builder:

Year Built:

Carriages:

Livery:

Operator:

Number:

Name:

Type:

Category:

Class:

Builder:

Year Built:

Carriages:

Livery:

Operator:

Number:

Name:

Type:

Category:

Class:

Builder:

Year Built:

Carriages:

Livery:

Operator: Number:

Name: Type:

Category: Class:

Builder: Year Built:

Carriages: Livery:

Operator: Number:

Name: Type:

Category: Class:

Builder: Year Built:

Carriages: Livery:

Operator: Number:

Name: Type:

Category: Class:

Builder: Year Built:

Carriages: Livery:

Operator: Number:

Name: Type:

Category: Class:

Builder: Year Built:

Carriages: Livery:

Operator: Number:

Name: Type:

Category: Class:

Builder: Year Built:

Carriages: Livery:

Operator: Number:

Name: Type:

Category: Class:

Builder: Year Built:

Carriages: Livery:

Operator: Number:

Name: Type:

Category: Class:

Builder: Year Built:

Carriages: Livery:

Operator: Number:

Name: Type:

Category: Class:

Builder: Year Built:

Carriages: Livery:

NOTES

LOCATION

Start Time: End Time:

Elapsed Time: Railway Line:

Location: County:

ROLLING STOCK

Operator: Number:

Name: Type:

Category: Class:

Builder: Year Built:

Carriages: Livery:

Operator: Number:

Name: Type:

Category: Class:

Builder: Year Built:

Carriages: Livery:

Operator: Number:

Name: Type:

Category: Class:

Builder: Year Built:

Carriages: Livery:

Operator:	Number:
Name:	Type:
Category:	Class:
Builder:	Year Built:
Carriages:	Livery:

Operator:	Number:
Name:	Type:
Category:	Class:
Builder:	Year Built:
Carriages:	Livery:

Operator:	Number:
Name:	Type:
Category:	Class:
Builder:	Year Built:
Carriages:	Livery:

Operator:	Number:
Name:	Type:
Category:	Class:
Builder:	Year Built:
Carriages:	Livery:

Operator: Number:

Name: Type:

Category: Class:

Builder: Year Built:

Carriages: Livery:

Operator: Number:

Name: Type:

Category: Class:

Builder: Year Built:

Carriages: Livery:

Operator: Number:

Name: Type:

Category: Class:

Builder: Year Built:

Carriages: Livery:

Operator: Number:

Name: Type:

Category: Class:

Builder: Year Built:

Carriages: Livery:

NOTES

LOCATION

Start Time:

End Time:

Elapsed Time:

Railway Line:

Location:

County:

ROLLING STOCK

Operator:

Number:

Name:

Type:

Category:

Class:

Builder:

Year Built:

Carriages:

Livery:

Operator:

Number:

Name:

Type:

Category:

Class:

Builder:

Year Built:

Carriages:

Livery:

Operator:

Number:

Name:

Type:

Category:

Class:

Builder:

Year Built:

Carriages:

Livery:

Operator: Number:

Name: Type:

Category: Class:

Builder: Year Built:

Carriages: Livery:

Operator: Number:

Name: Type:

Category: Class:

Builder: Year Built:

Carriages: Livery:

Operator: Number:

Name: Type:

Category: Class:

Builder: Year Built:

Carriages: Livery:

Operator: Number:

Name: Type:

Category: Class:

Builder: Year Built:

Carriages: Livery:

Operator: Number:

Name: Type:

Category: Class:

Builder: Year Built:

Carriages: Livery:

Operator: Number:

Name: Type:

Category: Class:

Builder: Year Built:

Carriages: Livery:

Operator: Number:

Name: Type:

Category: Class:

Builder: Year Built:

Carriages: Livery:

Operator: Number:

Name: Type:

Category: Class:

Builder: Year Built:

Carriages: Livery:

NOTES

LOCATION

Start Time: End Time:

Elapsed Time: Railway Line:

Location: County:

ROLLING STOCK

Operator: Number:

Name: Type:

Category: Class:

Builder: Year Built:

Carriages: Livery:

Operator: Number:

Name: Type:

Category: Class:

Builder: Year Built:

Carriages: Livery:

Operator: Number:

Name: Type:

Category: Class:

Builder: Year Built:

Carriages: Livery:

Operator: Number:

Name: Type:

Category: Class:

Builder: Year Built:

Carriages: Livery:

Operator: Number:

Name: Type:

Category: Class:

Builder: Year Built:

Carriages: Livery:

Operator: Number:

Name: Type:

Category: Class:

Builder: Year Built:

Carriages: Livery:

Operator: Number:

Name: Type:

Category: Class:

Builder: Year Built:

Carriages: Livery:

Operator: Number:

Name: Type:

Category: Class:

Builder: Year Built:

Carriages: Livery:

Operator: Number:

Name: Type:

Category: Class:

Builder: Year Built:

Carriages: Livery:

Operator: Number:

Name: Type:

Category: Class:

Builder: Year Built:

Carriages: Livery:

Operator: Number:

Name: Type:

Category: Class:

Builder: Year Built:

Carriages: Livery:

NOTES

M T W T F S S

LOCATION

Start Time:

End Time:

Elapsed Time:

Railway Line:

Location:

County:

ROLLING STOCK

Operator:

Number:

Name:

Type:

Category:

Class:

Builder:

Year Built:

Carriages:

Livery:

Operator:

Number:

Name:

Type:

Category:

Class:

Builder:

Year Built:

Carriages:

Livery:

Operator:

Number:

Name:

Type:

Category:

Class:

Builder:

Year Built:

Carriages:

Livery:

Operator: Number:

Name: Type:

Category: Class:

Builder: Year Built:

Carriages: Livery:

Operator: Number:

Name: Type:

Category: Class:

Builder: Year Built:

Carriages: Livery:

Operator: Number:

Name: Type:

Category: Class:

Builder: Year Built:

Carriages: Livery:

Operator: Number:

Name: Type:

Category: Class:

Builder: Year Built:

Carriages: Livery:

Operator: Number:

Name: Type:

Category: Class:

Builder: Year Built:

Carriages: Livery:

Operator: Number:

Name: Type:

Category: Class:

Builder: Year Built:

Carriages: Livery:

Operator: Number:

Name: Type:

Category: Class:

Builder: Year Built:

Carriages: Livery:

Operator: Number:

Name: Type:

Category: Class:

Builder: Year Built:

Carriages: Livery:

NOTES

LOCATION

Start Time: End Time:

Elapsed Time: Railway Line:

Location: County:

ROLLING STOCK

Operator: Number:

Name: Type:

Category: Class:

Builder: Year Built:

Carriages: Livery:

Operator: Number:

Name: Type:

Category: Class:

Builder: Year Built:

Carriages: Livery:

Operator: Number:

Name: Type:

Category: Class:

Builder: Year Built:

Carriages: Livery:

Operator: Number:

Name: Type:

Category: Class:

Builder: Year Built:

Carriages: Livery:

Operator: Number:

Name: Type:

Category: Class:

Builder: Year Built:

Carriages: Livery:

Operator: Number:

Name: Type:

Category: Class:

Builder: Year Built:

Carriages: Livery:

Operator: Number:

Name: Type:

Category: Class:

Builder: Year Built:

Carriages: Livery:

Operator: Number:

Name: Type:

Category: Class:

Builder: Year Built:

Carriages: Livery:

Operator: Number:

Name: Type:

Category: Class:

Builder: Year Built:

Carriages: Livery:

Operator: Number:

Name: Type:

Category: Class:

Builder: Year Built:

Carriages: Livery:

Operator: Number:

Name: Type:

Category: Class:

Builder: Year Built:

Carriages: Livery:

NOTES

LOCATION

Start Time: End Time:

Elapsed Time: Railway Line:

Location: County:

ROLLING STOCK

Operator: Number:

Name: Type:

Category: Class:

Builder: Year Built:

Carriages: Livery:

Operator: Number:

Name: Type:

Category: Class:

Builder: Year Built:

Carriages: Livery:

Operator: Number:

Name: Type:

Category: Class:

Builder: Year Built:

Carriages: Livery:

Operator: Number:

Name: Type:

Category: Class:

Builder: Year Built:

Carriages: Livery:

Operator: Number:

Name: Type:

Category: Class:

Builder: Year Built:

Carriages: Livery:

Operator: Number:

Name: Type:

Category: Class:

Builder: Year Built:

Carriages: Livery:

Operator: Number:

Name: Type:

Category: Class:

Builder: Year Built:

Carriages: Livery:

Operator: Number:

Name: Type:

Category: Class:

Builder: Year Built:

Carriages: Livery:

Operator: Number:

Name: Type:

Category: Class:

Builder: Year Built:

Carriages: Livery:

Operator: Number:

Name: Type:

Category: Class:

Builder: Year Built:

Carriages: Livery:

Operator: Number:

Name: Type:

Category: Class:

Builder: Year Built:

Carriages: Livery:

NOTES

LOCATION

Start Time:

End Time:

Elapsed Time:

Railway Line:

Location:

County:

ROLLING STOCK

Operator:

Number:

Name:

Type:

Category:

Class:

Builder:

Year Built:

Carriages:

Livery:

Operator:

Number:

Name:

Type:

Category:

Class:

Builder:

Year Built:

Carriages:

Livery:

Operator:

Number:

Name:

Type:

Category:

Class:

Builder:

Year Built:

Carriages:

Livery:

Operator: Number:

Name: Type:

Category: Class:

Builder: Year Built:

Carriages: Livery:

Operator: Number:

Name: Type:

Category: Class:

Builder: Year Built:

Carriages: Livery:

Operator: Number:

Name: Type:

Category: Class:

Builder: Year Built:

Carriages: Livery:

Operator: Number:

Name: Type:

Category: Class:

Builder: Year Built:

Carriages: Livery:

Operator: Number:

Name: Type:

Category: Class:

Builder: Year Built:

Carriages: Livery:

Operator: Number:

Name: Type:

Category: Class:

Builder: Year Built:

Carriages: Livery:

Operator: Number:

Name: Type:

Category: Class:

Builder: Year Built:

Carriages: Livery:

Operator: Number:

Name: Type:

Category: Class:

Builder: Year Built:

Carriages: Livery:

NOTES